D1489182

FASHION QUOTES

STYLISH WIT & CATWALK WISDOM

ILLUSTRATIONS BY CHRISTIAN LACROIX

FASHION QUOTES

STYLISH WIT & CATWALK WISDOM

Patrick Mauriès & Jean-Christophe Napias

Thames & Hudson

CONTENTS

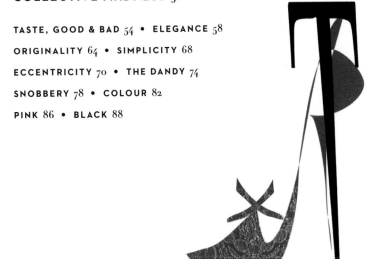

PROLOGUE

Fashion has only one enemy: nature. It belongs entirely
to the realm of the artificial, the imaginary and the sublime.
Its sole aim is to provide an alternative to reality and offer
a way of fixing its faults. Although fashion has existed since
ancient times, it was not until many centuries later that it
was described in the most refined terms by the aesthetes and
intellects of the late 19th century, from Poe and Baudelaire
to Wilde and Mallarmé, who were all united by the same
obsession with the ideal and by the rejection of what
Baudelaire described in his essay *In Praise of Make-Up* as 'all
that natural life accumulates that is coarse, earthly and foul'.
From trinkets to trimmings, fashion's role is not merely to
mend the mistakes of nature, but to create a version of nature
that is exaggerated, elevated, exciting, and quite literally
extraordinary. As Baudelaire's definition of a woman states,
'as an idol, she must adorn herself in order to be adored' .

That phrase is a textbook example of how fashion
provides the ideal raw material for all kinds of decrees, edicts,
maxims, definitive pronouncements, clever quips and cutting
remarks. These emanate not only from the upper echelons
of literature and the heavenly havens of fashion magazines
and their eminent oracles, but often from celebrities whose
media ubiquity may be no guarantee of artistic worth but is
nonetheless enough to make them arbiters of taste.

It was a long time ago that fashion first broke free from
the inner circles of elite patrons and elegant authors and began
to take an increasingly important place in the culture and
imagination of broader societies who all idolize the same

cult brands and style icons – terms that themselves have migrated from the realm of religion to the realm of retail.

It could be argued that late 19th-century society survived well into the 1960s, with luminaries such as Marcel Proust, to name but one, bridging the gap between the Decadent and Symbolist movements and the fashionable world whose brightest lights – Jean Cocteau, Cecil Beaton, Louise de Vilmorin, Nancy Mitford – were still glowing in the late sixties. In the wake of this era came the jet set of the 1970s, where art mingled cheerfully with high fashion and high society, with figures like the aquiline Diana Vreeland, the sardonic Truman Capote and the taciturn Andy Warhol, as well as couturiers and designers including Yves Saint Laurent and Karl Lagerfeld as part of the glittering scene.

In the decades that followed, the great fashion houses were taken over by a handful of powerful corporations, a situation that did little to encourage free thinking or free speech beyond the fixed boundaries of brand names and advertising slogans, carefully constructed and constantly repeated. Nevertheless, some designers have managed to retain their sense of fun and cultivate an appealing inventiveness and lightness of touch, as have a handful of stars, fashion bloggers and fashion lovers old and new.

The following pages are a tribute to the fashion world's inexhaustible creativity with words. Taken from many eras and cultures, across a wealth of changing styles and trends, these quotes reflect a great historical and linguistic diversity and showcase the wit that has grown from such frivolous yet fertile ground.

PM

What is
FASHION?

Fashion is what one **WEARS** oneself. What is unfashionable is what **OTHER** people wear.

Oscar Wilde

The truly fashionable are beyond fashion.
Cecil Beaton

It was Colley Cibber who said that one might as well be out
of the world as be out of fashion. But far more important than
being stylish or passé is the question of our attitude towards
fashion. Those who disregard it completely are the losers, for
they miss the delightful multiplicity and charm of the fads
that reflect our deepest psychological needs. He who ignores
fashion ignores life itself.
Cecil Beaton

Fashion journals don't teach you how to be beautiful.
What does fashion have to do with you? So don't give
it any thought, and simply wear what suits you.
Paul Poiret

Women hold fashion dear because novelty always
reflects youth.
Madeleine de Scudéry

Silly women follow fashion, pretentious ones overdo it,
but women of taste come to a good-natured accord with it.
Émilie de Breteuil, Marquise du Châtelet

Fashion is nothing but an induced epidemic.
George Bernard Shaw

Fashion is the ЯОЯЯIM of HISTORY.

Louis XIV of France

In fashion, the only certainty is that nothing is certain.

Kenzo Takada

Fashion should be a game.

Mary Quant

Fashion should therefore be considered as a symptom
of the love for the ideal that floats in the human brain above
all that natural life accumulates that is coarse, earthly and
foul, like a sublime deformation of nature, or rather a series
of unceasing and successive attempts to reform nature.

Charles Baudelaire

Must I make myself a slave to fashion
And not dress for my own sake?

Molière, *The School of Husbands*, Act 1, Scene 1

If you are not in fashion, you are nobody.

Lord Chesterfield

Fashion anticipates.

Oleg Cassini

Fashion: the search for a new absurdity.

Natalie Clifford Barney

With Pierre Cardin, I learned you can make a hat with a chair.

Jean Paul Gaultier

In difficult times fashion is always outrageous.

Elsa Schiaparelli

Why is the art of fashion left entirely to the whims of tailors
and dressmakers, in a civilization in which clothes are
extremely important because morality and the climate mean
that nudity is never seen? In modern times, clothes have
become a sort of skin for man, which he never removes under
any circumstances and which sticks to him like the hide of an
animal, to the point that nowadays, the true shape of the body
has long been forgotten.

Théophile Gautier

I want to stop using the term fashion, because Eve made
Adam bite an apple. Since then, it's been illegal to be naked.
I'm helping people follow the law in style.

Kanye West

Men often design absurd fashions in order to take revenge
on women.

Roland Barthes

Prejudice is a disease. So is fashion. But I will not wear
prejudice.

Lady Gaga

Fashion is not beautiful, neither is it ugly. Why should
it be either? Fashion is fashion.

Anna Wintour

One could perhaps divide the hierarchy of fashion into three ranks: those who play fashion's game and are the sheep; those who play the game and are the leaders; and lastly, the real shepherds, who, though they avoid or eschew active participation, cannot help being fashionable because of the authority with which they express their tastes.

Cecil Beaton

Fashion is everywhere. Everywhere! Flowers are fashion to me, the sky is fashion, my garden is fashion. My darling, the Sistine Chapel is fashion.

Anna Dello Russo

Enjoy your life, fashion is not that important.

Dries Van Noten

If you can't eat it, it's not food, and if you can't wear it, it's not fashion, it is something else.

Alber Elbaz

Fashion constantly begins and ends in the two things it abhors most, singularity and vulgarity.

William Hazlitt

Fashion guides society. Therefore the couturier should not be denied a say in the aesthetic domain.

Paul Poiret

I don't approach fashion; fashion approaches me.

Daphne Guinness

Each fashion season, with all its latest designs, gives secret
signals of things to come. Whoever might be able to read them
would not only know in advance new art movements, but also
laws, wars and new revolutions. That, without doubt, is where
the greatest attraction of fashion may be found, but there also
lies the difficulty that it has to exploit.

Walter Benjamin

Fashion is gentility running away from vulgarity and afraid
of being overtaken.

William Hazlitt

There's no more fashion, just clothes.

Karl Lagerfeld

There is something about fashion that can make people
really nervous.

Anna Wintour

Fashion is what **YOU** adopt when **YOU** don't know who **YOU** are.

Quentin Crisp

What is
STYLE?

Fashions FADE, style is ETERNAL.

Yves Saint Laurent

Style is a way to say who you are without having to speak.
Rachel Zoe

The coolest thing is when you don't care about being cool anymore. Indifference is the greatest aphrodisiac: that's what really sums up style for me.
Rick Owens

Fashion is what you're offered four times a year by designers. And style is what you choose.
Lauren Hutton

Style as a concept has been hijacked to mean elite, refined and expensive when it should be thought of as a basic expression of life in much the same way as we all identify with music or speech.
Scott Schuman

If you're too big to fit into fashion, then you just have to do your own fashion.
Vivienne Westwood

It's all proportion, and line... that's all fashion is – line, and dash. STYLE is the great thing. Oh you gotta have style! It helps you get up in the morning! It helps you get down the stairs!
Diana Vreeland, as portrayed in Mark Hampton and
Mary Louise Wilson's play *Full Gallop*

WHY change?
Everyone has
their **OWN**
style. When
you have found
it, you should
STICK to it.

Audrey Hepburn

There are sometimes people, or things, possessed of an invisible charm, a natural grace, that is impossible to define, and that one is forced to call the *je ne sais quoi.*

Montesquieu

You're certainly no beauty, but you have something much much better. You have style.

Frieda Loehmann to Iris Apfel

Fashion you can buy, but style you possess. The key to style is learning who you are, which takes years. There's no how-to road map to style. It's about self-expression and, above all, attitude.

Iris Apfel

Style is wearing an evening dress to McDonald's, wearing heels to play football. It is personality, confidence and seduction.

John Galliano

Fashion is what people tell you to wear. Style is what comes from your own inner thing.

Pauline Trigère

Style begins by looking good naked. It's a discipline. And if you don't dress well every day, you lose the habit. It's not about what you wear, but about how you live your life.

Oscar de la Renta

Style doesn't have seasons.

Polly Allen Mellen

Style is having the courage of one's choices and the courage
to say no. It's good taste and culture.

Giorgio Armani

Fashion is a way of not having to decide who you are.
Style is deciding who you are and being able to perpetuate it.

Quentin Crisp

The essence of style is a simple way of saying
something complex.

Giorgio Armani

Talent and taste are not enough. Only style counts.

Pierre Cardin

You can have anything you want in life if you dress for it.

Edith Head

The
NECESSARY
and the
Superfluous

FASHION
becomes
unfashionable.
STYLE never.

Coco Chanel

ARTIFICE

The ultimate trick is to appear natural. But sublimely natural.

Paul Poiret

The look of being too deliberately dressed, with everything
cautiously matching, always bores me.

Babe Paley

The first duty in life is to be as artificial as possible.
Give me the luxuries and I can dispense with the necessities.

Oscar Wilde

BEAUTY

Beauty is like a sunset: it goes as soon as you try to capture it.
The beauty you like is precisely that which escapes you.

Issey Miyake

For something to be beautiful it doesn't have to be pretty.

Rei Kawakubo

Beauty isn't something pretty-pretty: why do so many mothers
teach their daughters to do nothing but mince about, instead
of teaching them about beauty? It's true, beauty can't be taught
all at once; but by the time one has understood that, beauty
has gone! That's part of the drama of being a woman.

Coco Chanel

I know what women want. They want to be beautiful.

Valentino Garavani

I believe that there are three conditions to a woman's beauty.
First, you must realize that not all women are beautiful all of
the time. Sometimes beauty comes on a subconscious level.
When she is in love, or has met someone new and exciting,
she shines. Second, you must understand that life is unfair.
Beauty is something that, for some, must be worked at.
The third condition is luck. Some women can just be lucky.

Yohji Yamamoto

Fashion itself and countries decide on what can
be called beauty.

Blaise Pascal

You don't have to be born beautiful to be wildly attractive.

Diana Vreeland

Everything that is beautiful can live together.

Roger Vivier

There are no **UGLY** women, only **LAZY** ones.

Helena Rubinstein

CHIC

All a woman needs to be chic is a raincoat, two suits,
a pair of trousers and a cashmere sweater.

Hubert de Givenchy

Chic is no longer synonymous with elegance...
The new fashion is unconstrained, bold, solid and realist.

Vogue, 1936

The sporty silhouette is absolute chic.

Jean Patou

'Good taste' is banal. Eccentricity is chic.

Jean Paul Gaultier

Le freak, c'est chic.

Chic

You cannot fake chic but you can be chic and fake fur.

Karl Lagerfeld

We don't want to be chic; we just want to be ridiculous.

Marion Foale and Sally Tuffin

HAUTE COUTURE

Haute couture is a mass of whispered secrets.
Rare are those who have the privilege of passing them on.

Yves Saint Laurent

Haute couture is like opera: it is a ritual. It is refinement.
Couture doesn't improvise. It is connected to a memory,
to craftsmanship, and to expert knowledge.

Emanuel Ungaro

Haute couture lets women rediscover a figure that age
has made them lose.

Charles James

I only believe in haute couture. In my opinion, a couturier
must establish his style and stick to it. Too many couturiers
make the mistake of wanting to change their line for every
collection. Personally, I change a little every time, but never
too much, so as not to lose my identity.

Valentino Garavani

Insofar as one can talk of a Vionnet school, it comes mostly
from my having been an enemy of fashion. There is something
superficial and volatile about the seasonal and elusive whims
of fashion which offends my sense of beauty.

Madeleine Vionnet

Haute couture should be **FUN, FOOLISH** and **ALMOST** unwearable.

Christian Lacroix

It is necessary, you see, to raise couture to a sort of apostolate. Because it is so purely French, it must be a perfect expression of French genius in terms of restraint, taste and quality. Because couture is devoted to women, it must glorify women and compose a real poem with every garment they wear.

Madeleine Vionnet

Real couture is not taking a piece of chiffon and stitching it into a flower, it's knowing how to match bias to grain.

Hubert de Givenchy

LUXURY

The media is constantly redefining what luxury is.
Luxury can be a dirty sock if dressed up in the right way.

Zac Posen

Luxury is less expensive than elegance.

Honoré de Balzac

Luxury to me is not about buying expensive things;
it's about living in a way where you appreciate things.

Oscar de la Renta

DESIGNERS

The most important thing you should know about me is that not everything you're told by others is necessarily the truth.

Karl Lagerfeld

Do I make fashion mistakes? Yes, but I won't say what.

Domenico Dolce

I could never live without artwork. It's a constant inspiration.

Narciso Rodriguez

I have so many fashion mistakes, but that's part of being in fashion. I think the people that you see make the most mistakes are usually the best dressers.

Zac Posen

I remember a designer who said her dresses were worn only by intelligent women. Of course she went bankrupt.

Karl Lagerfeld

Coco Chanel gave women freedom. Yves Saint Laurent gave them power. He left aesthetic territory behind in order to explore social territory. He created a body of work with a social impact.

Pierre Bergé

The hardest thing in fashion is not to be known for a logo, but to be known for a silhouette.

Giambattista Valli

I could say that my work is about looking for accidents.
Accidents are quite important for me. Something is new
because it is an accident.

Rei Kawakubo

I am what is popularly regarded as the greatest couturier
in the western world.

Charles James

For us, fashion is an antidote to reality.

Viktor & Rolf

A designer is like a doctor for a woman. He has a specific job,
and if he is doing it well, he will have the gratitude of the
woman for the rest of his life.

Oleg Cassini

I am trying to work out which images of the female I want
to analyse. I'm not really interested in clothes or style.

Miuccia Prada

Couture is crazy, contradictory, unpredictable and above all,
more powerful than me.

Christian Lacroix

The clothes I prefer are the ones I invent for a life that doesn't
exist yet, the world of tomorrow.

Pierre Cardin

All my dresses come from a gesture. A dress that doesn't reflect or make you think of a gesture is no good.

Yves Saint Laurent

My measure is excess.

Thierry Mugler

Fashion, no. I prefer clothes. One can always be in fashion.

agnès b.

I made clothes that looked like ruins. I created something new by destroying the old. This wasn't fashion as a commodity, this was fashion as an idea.

Malcolm McLaren

There is nothing worse that being the designer of the moment, because one day that moment passes.

Alber Elbaz

There is nothing new except what has been forgotten.

Rose Bertin

I've always thought of the T-shirt as the Alpha and Omega of the fashion alphabet.

Giorgio Armani

I like to push at limits, and I'm obsessed with line. Any less wouldn't be enough; any more would be too much.

Anthony Vaccarello

All my inspiration has always come from my childhood.

Jean-Charles de Castelbajac

I am happy to have given some well-deserved credibility
to the humble craft of shoemaker.

Salvatore Ferragamo

I'm not a designer; designers are hired help that only copy
what's on the wind. They don't create fashion. Only a couturier
does this, with his client as inspiration.

Charles James

When I started my own business, my main reason for
designing clothes was that I wanted to dress rock stars and
the people who went to rock concerts. It didn't go beyond
that aspiration at that point.

Anna Sui

Derision is one of my big motivators.

Jean Paul Gaultier

A couturier dresses human beings, not dreams.

Madeleine Vionnet

I don't design CLOTHES. I design DREAMS.

Ralph Lauren

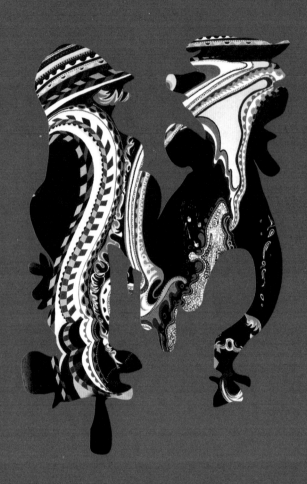

MATERIALS

I do not believe in God. I believe in cashmere.

Fran Lebowitz

My mother was right: When you've got nothing left, all you
can do is get into silk underwear and start reading Proust.

Jane Birkin

Fabric is where everything begins, the prerequisite
of all inspiration.

Hubert de Givenchy

To work with beautiful materials is a true pleasure.
And one must take pleasure in creation.

Christophe Josse

With one or ten metres of fabric, you dress a living being,
and the piece of fabric itself comes to life too.

Hubert de Givenchy

One cannot contradict cloth.

Cristóbal Balenciaga

ART & FASHION

Dressing is a science, an art, a habit and a feeling
all at once.

Honoré de Balzac

Fashion as art is contrived. Designing clothes is working-class:
I'm working-class.

Karl Lagerfeld

Am I a fool to dream of putting art into my dresses,
am I mad to say that couture is an art?

Paul Poiret

Art cannot do anything for fashion. If fashion is sometimes
used by art, that is good enough for the glory of fashion.

Marcel Rochas

For myself, fashion is not a craft but an art.

Elsa Schiaparelli

Art is cerebral. When I make clothes I think, of course.
But the result is something beautiful that one feels good
in, not a dogma.

Guillaume Henry

As a fashion designer, I was always aware that I was not
an artist, because I was creating something that was made
to be sold, marketed, used, and ultimately discarded.

Tom Ford

Clothes that are not worn are of no interest. Dresses are not made for museums.

Michel Klein

I spent my life making fashion an art form.

Charles James

A dress is not a tragedy, nor is it a painting.

Coco Chanel

Fashion is only the attempt to realize art in living forms and social intercourse.

Oliver Wendell Holmes

Fashion is a craft and an expression of a period of time but it is not an art. It's pretentious to be in awe of it.

Bill Blass

Certain dressmakers desire to pass for an artist. I have one ambition: that is to have good taste.

Jean Patou

Whenever I sign a garment with my name, I consider myself the creator of a masterpiece.

Paul Poiret

At a time fashion has become an art that embodies all other art forms, a fashion magazine must also be a journal of art. This is what *La Gazette du Bon Ton* will be!

Lucien Vogel

Fashion is an art form – you might call it decorative or applied art as opposed to fine art, but what's the distinction? Because the same amount of artistic expression goes into clothes, a piece of pottery or a painting.

Zandra Rhodes

One should either be a work of art, or wear a work of art.

Oscar Wilde

Personal
Taste, Collective
MADNESS

I prefer **BAD** taste to **NO** taste.

John Galliano

TASTE, GOOD & BAD

The intoxicating thing about bad taste is the aristocratic pleasure of giving offence.

Charles Baudelaire

Every era gets the bad taste it deserves.

Karl Lagerfeld

Ugly is attractive, ugly is exciting. Maybe because it is newer. The investigation of ugliness is, to me, more interesting than the bourgeois idea of beauty. And why? Because ugly is human.

Miuccia Prada

It's always the badly dressed people who are the most interesting.

Jean Paul Gaultier

It is the fashions that seem most hostile to current taste at the time which last the longest when they end up being successful.

Octave Uzanne

I'm all about exuberance. We only have one short life to live, and we shouldn't waste it being tasteful.

Isaac Mizrahi

Jogging pants are a sign of defeat. You've lost control of your life, so you go out in jogging pants.

Karl Lagerfeld

If I had the power, I would ban leggings.

Jil Sander

Flip flops are a gateway drug, the downfall of many relationships.
Lady Gaga

Taste is something that allows us to distinguish the beautiful from the ugly, the elegant from the vulgar; it lends all our actions and our least movements an inexplicable charm.
Montesquieu

Taste is the feeling that permits one to tell the difference between what is beautiful and what is merely spectacular.
Madeleine Vionnet

Dressing well is a form of good manners.
Tom Ford

Bad taste means confusing fashion, which exists only through change, with lasting beauty.
Stendhal

A little bad taste is like a nice splash of paprika. We all need a splash of bad taste – it's hearty, it's healthy, it's physical. I think we could use more of it. No taste is what I'm against.
Diana Vreeland

Good taste is death. Vulgarity is life.
Mary Quant

You have to want to have taste. Some people have inherently bad taste. Their problem is really not the bad taste – that can be fixed – but that they don't know they have it!

Carrie Donovan

Too much good taste can be boring.

Diana Vreeland

If you put something together and it doesn't look so good, the fashion police are not going to come and take you away. And if they do, you might have some fun in jail.

Iris Apfel

ELEGANCE

To be truly elegant, one should not be noticed.

Beau Brummell

The most important thing about elegance is that it should hide its methods. Everything that smacks of economy lacks elegance.

Honoré de Balzac

Fashion is a passing thing – a thing of fancy, fantasy and feeling. Elegance is innate. It has nothing to do with being well-dressed. It's a quality possessed by certain thoughts and certain animals. Gazelles, I suppose, have elegance with their tiny heads and their satiny coats and their little winning ways... So I said: gazelles have elegance. And Audrey Hepburn, magnificently.

Diana Vreeland

What is elegance? Soap and water.

Cecil Beaton

The greatest elegance is truth.

Thierry Mugler

Luxury is a matter of money. Elegance is a question of education.

Sacha Guitry

What a woman reads makes her more attractive and more elegant than what she wears.

Carine Roitfeld

Isn't elegance forgetting what one is wearing?

Yves Saint Laurent

Forced elegance is to true elegance what a wig is to hair.

Honoré de Balzac

The woman with elegance skilfully conceals the coarseness of desire; her garb is contrived to make her desirable, but she knows how to retain the artlessness of modesty, the grace of reserve; she shows what she hides, and hides what she shows.

Henri-Frédéric Amiel

Elegance is good taste plus a dash of daring.

Carmel Snow

Elegance doesn't mean being noticed, it means being remembered.

Giorgio Armani

Elegance is the only beauty that never fades.

Audrey Hepburn

Elegance is being equally beautiful inside and outside.

Coco Chanel

Elegance is a progressive concept.

Hedi Slimane

Elegance is a physical quality. If a woman doesn't have it naked, she'll never have it clothed.

Karl Lagerfeld

An elegant woman is a woman who despises you and has no hair under her arms.

Salvador Dalí

The only real elegance is in the mind; if you've got that, the rest really comes from it.

Diana Vreeland

Elegance is a discipline of life.

Oscar de la Renta

Elegance is the balance between proportion, emotion and surprise.

Valentino Garavani

Elegance is more than grace and less than beauty. Why could it not be, for example, the notion of beauty expressed in little things and raised above the simple notion of prettiness?

Jules Barbey d'Aurevilly

Elegance must be the right combination of distinction, naturalness, care and simplicity. Outside this, believe me, there is no elegance. Only pretension.

Christian Dior

A woman is always too dressed, never too elegant.

Coco Chanel

Real elegance, which is always personal and restrained,
is a form of freedom founded on self-knowledge.

Louise de Vilmorin

You can't learn how to be elegant; you can only learn how to
avoid mistakes. The rest is instinct. Elegance is about the way
you cross your legs, not the label or the newest clothes from
the latest collection.

Carine Roitfeld

Without elegance of the heart, there is no elegance.

Yves Saint Laurent

Then I said something I've always known. I don't know who
it's a quote from. I didn't get it from you, shall we say, and
I didn't make it up, but I've known it all my life. Elegance,
I said, is refusal.

Diana Vreeland

When I hear old **FOOLS** say elegance is **DEAD**, I tell them: no it's not, its face has changed.

Karl Lagerfeld

ORIGINALITY

You weren't mass-produced, so be unique.

Manolo Blahnik

To be irreplaceable, you must be different.

Coco Chanel

When you don't dress like everybody else, you don't have
to think like everybody else.

Iris Apfel

The idea of seeing everybody clad the same is not really
my cup of tea.

Christian Lacroix

I always wear my sweater back to front, it is much
more flattering.

Diana Vreeland

Be daring, be different, be impractical; be anything that will
assert integrity of purpose and imaginative vision against the
play-it-safers, the creatures of the commonplace, the slaves
of the ordinary.

Cecil Beaton

Beware of originality: in couture one soon falls straight
into disguise and decorativeness, one blends into the decor.

Coco Chanel

STYLE —
all who have it
share **ONE** thing:
originality.

Diana Vreeland

Women of the world today dress alike. They are like so many loaves of bread. To be beautiful one must be unhurried. Personality is needed. There is too much sameness. The world seems only to have a desire for more of this sameness. To be different is to be alone.

Luisa Casati

In fashion, there are so many gangs, if you identify too much with one, you get caught – I would lose my freedom.

Daphne Guinness

SIMPLICITY

In character, in manners, in style, in all things, the supreme excellence is simplicity.

Henry Wadsworth Longfellow

Perfection in dress consists of absolute simplicity, which is actually the best way to distinguish oneself.

Charles Baudelaire

For a dress to be able to survive from one era to the next, it must be imbued with extreme purity.

Madame Grès

Any excess in fashion is a sign of the end.

Paul Poiret

ECCENTRICITY

Eccentricity exists particularly in the English, and partly, I think, because of that peculiar and satisfactory knowledge of infallibility that is the hallmark and birthright of the British nation.

Edith Sitwell

I was never hurt by what anybody said about my clothes, because I dress to please myself. If somebody doesn't like what I'm wearing, it's their problem, not mine.

Iris Apfel

Eccentricity is not, as dull people would have us believe, a form of madness. It is often a kind of innocent pride, and the man of genius and the aristocrat are frequently regarded as eccentrics because genius and aristocrat are entirely unafraid of and uninfluenced by the opinions and vagaries of the crowd.

Edith Sitwell

It follows from all this that one of the consequences of Dandyism, one of its principal characteristics – or rather its character in more general terms – is always to produce the unexpected. ...Eccentricity, another fruit of the English soil, leads to the same thing, though this time in a blind, wild, unbridled way.

Jules Barbey d'Aurevilly

Moderation is a fatal thing. Nothing succeeds like excess.

Oscar Wilde

To go further in our search for some antidote against
melancholy, we may seek in our dust-heap for some rigid,
and even splendid, attitude of Death, some exaggeration of
the attitudes common to Life. This attitude, rigidity, protest,
or explanation, has been called eccentricity by those whose
bones are too pliant.

Edith Sitwell

I **ONLY** like eccentricity in **OTHER** people.

Coco Chanel

THE DANDY

The dandy's achievement is simply to be himself.

William Hazlitt

A Dandy is a clothes-wearing Man, a Man whose trade, office
and existence consists in the wearing of Clothes. Every faculty
of his soul, spirit, purse, and person is heroically consecrated
to this one object, the wearing of Clothes wisely and well:
so that the others dress to live, he lives to dress.

Thomas Carlyle

Dandyism is a heresy of the elegant life.

Honoré de Balzac

Dandyism, contrary to what many people believe without
thinking, is not even an immoderate taste for clothes and
material elegance. For the dandy these things are no more
than a symbol of the aristocratic superiority of his mind.

Charles Baudelaire

True dandyism is the result of an artistic temperament
working upon a fine body within the wide limits of fashion.

Max Beerbohm

Dandyism is a variety of genius.

William Hazlitt

The distinguishing quality of the dandy's beauty primarily
consists of the air of coldness that comes from his unshakeable
resolution to remain unmoved.

Charles Baudelaire

What defines the dandy is independence.

Jules Barbey d'Aurevilly

Nothing goes against the rules of high dandyism more than
to recognize, in surprise or admiration, that one is inferior
to something.

Théophile Gautier

Dandyism is almost as difficult a thing to describe as it is to
define. Those who see things only from a narrow point of view
have imagined it to be especially the art of dress, a bold and
felicitous dictatorship in the matter of clothes and exterior
elegance. That it most certainly is, but much more besides.
Dandyism is a complete theory of life and its material is not
its only side. It is a way of existing, made up entirely of shades.

Jules Barbey d'Aurevilly

A man who can dominate a London dinner table can dominate
the world. The future belongs to the dandy.

Oscar Wilde

Brummel wore gloves that moulded themselves to his hands
like wet muslin. But dandyism lay not in the perfection of
these gloves, which outlined the nails just like flesh did;
it lay in the fact that they were made by four specialist artists:
three for the hand, one for the thumb.

Jules Barbey d'Aurevilly

Dandyism means adopting the point of view of the
housekeeper who will find the corpse in the morning.

Frédéric Berthet

The famous maxim of the dandy: 'in society, as long as you have made no impression, stay; once the impression is made, go.'

Jules Barbey d'Aurevilly

The dandy, therefore, is always compelled to astonish. Singularity is his vocation, excess his way to perfection. Perpetually incomplete, always on the fringe of things, he compels others to create him, while denying their values. He plays at life because he is unable to live it. He plays at it until he dies, except for the moments he is alone and without a mirror. For the dandy, to be alone is not to exist. The romantics only talked so grandly about solitude because it was their real horror, the one thing they could not bear.

Albert Camus

Every dandy is a daredevil, but a daredevil with tact, who stops in time and who finds, between originality and eccentricity, Pascal's famous point of intersection.

Jules Barbey d'Aurevilly

Dandyism is the last burst of heroism in a time of decadence.

Charles Baudelaire

To inoculate all of contemporary clothing, via Fashion, with a bit of dandyism was always going to kill dandyism itself since, in its very essence, dandyism was always condemned to be radical or not exist at all. ...It really is Fashion that has killed dandyism.

Roland Barthes

SNOBBERY

One must lack wit in order not to be a snob.

Robert de Montesquiou

Even the sound of the word 'snob', starting with a whistle and
ending with a soap bubble, meant it was destined for a great
career in scorn and frivolity.

Philippe Jullian

First, the World was made: then, as a matter of course, Snobs;
they existed for years and years, and were no more known
than America.

William Makepeace Thackeray

I'm a snob... I'm a snob
I've been bitten by the bug
I always crash in Jaguars
I spend August in bed
Small details of that sort
Make you a snob or not
I'm a snob... Even more snobbish than before
And when I die
I want a shroud from chez Dior!

Boris Vian, *J'suis snob*

As I have lived since the age of fifteen in the midst of ladies like the Mmes de Guermantes, I have the strength to risk the opinion that I am a snob, in the eyes of those who know no better, by depicting snobbery not from the outside and ironically, as would a novelist who was a snob, but from the inside, by forcing myself to take on the soul of someone who would like to know a Duchesse de Guermantes.

Marcel Proust

Snobbery is to fashion what condiments are to cooking. They add spice, flavour, something extra that enhances, irritates or delights but never leaves one indifferent.

Francis de Miomandre

I jog in Lanvin.

Kanye West

We must NEVER confuse elegance with snobbery.

Yves Saint Laurent

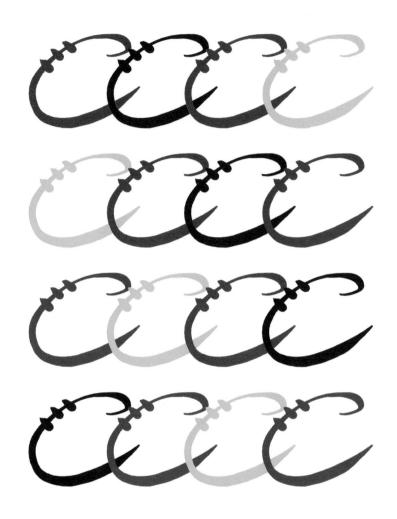

COLOUR

Black and white might be sufficient. But why deprive
yourself of colour?

Christian Dior

When in doubt wear red.

Bill Blass

Red: I've realized that after black and white, there is no
finer colour.

Valentino Garavani

Red is the great clarifier – bright, cleansing and revealing.
It makes all other colours beautiful. I can't imagine becoming
bored with red – it would be like becoming bored with the
person you love.

Diana Vreeland

My work is made of colours structured around white,
the translation of light, azure, the translation of the cosmos,
and silver, the reflection of light.

André Courrèges

Gaiety is one of the most important elements I brought
to fashion. I brought it through colour.

Emilio Pucci

I shall retire into dove colour and old lavender with a lace
collar and lawn wristlets.

Virginia Woolf

Red is the **ULTIMATE CURE** for sadness.

Bill Blass

Colour depends entirely on the tonality. Green for instance can look like the subway – but if you get the right green... A spring green, for instance, is marvellous. The green of England and the green of France are the most beautiful spring greens. The green of England is a little deeper than the green of France, a little darker...

Diana Vreeland

In all things, a multiplicity of colours means bad taste.

Honoré de Balzac

Me, I adore colour. I'm going to make dresses that sing, suits that play with the rainbow, coats that make little spots of light on the Champs-Elysées.

Guy Laroche

I'm always happy when I have a monochromatic outfit that isn't black, and that usually takes like seven years' worth of shopping to get right.

Kanye West

PINK

I always tell this story: When I started, the woman went to the store to buy a dress. She saw it in pink and red, and then she remembered that the husband, who is probably going to pay for the dress, loves it in pink. So she buys the pink. Today, the same woman goes to the store and remembers the husband likes pink, and she buys the red.

Oscar de la Renta

Rose is the navy blue of India.

Diana Vreeland

Banish the black! Burn the blue! And bury the beige!…
Think pink!

Miss Prescott (a caricature of Diana Vreeland) in *Funny Face* (1957)

Think pink, as Diana Vreeland said.
But don't wear it!

Karl Lagerfeld

BLACK

I think in black.

Gareth Pugh

To be beautiful, a woman needs nothing but a black pullover,
a black skirt, and the man she loves by her side.

Yves Saint Laurent

Women think of all colours except the absence of colour.
I have said that black has it all. White too. Their beauty is
absolute. It is the perfect harmony.

Coco Chanel

People dress in black because it doesn't show the dirt. They
put on dirty clothes every morning. Modern life demands
cleanliness, inside and out.

André Courrèges

Black is the most slimming of all colours. It is the most
flattering. You can wear black at any time. You can wear
it at any age. You may wear it for almost any occasion.
I could write a book about black.

Christian Dior

Black is modest and arrogant at the same time. Black is lazy
and easy – but mysterious. But, above all, black says this:
'I don't bother you – don't bother me.'

Yohji Yamamoto

I work in three shades of black.

Rei Kawakubo

Medvedenko: Why do you always wear black?
Masha: I'm in mourning for my life.

Anton Chekhov, *The Seagull*

It's really easy to get colours right. It's really hard to get black
– and neutrals – right. Black is certainly a colour but it's also
an illusion.

Donna Karan

Black is not sad... Black is poetic.

Ann Demeulemeester

I like black, because for me it is a very happy colour.

Azzedine Alaïa

Black and white always look modern, whatever that
word means.

Karl Lagerfeld

I love black because it affirms, designs and styles.
A woman in a black dress is a pencil stroke.

Yves Saint Laurent

People think that *everyone* wears black in France; in fact they *all* wear **GREY.**

Jean Paul Gaultier

Accessories &
FRIPPERIES

The **LESS** you can afford for your frocks, the **MORE** care you *must* take with your accessories.

Christian Dior

ESSENTIALS

If there was a choice on spending a lot of money on accessories
or dress, I always chose accessories.

Iris Apfel

The best fashion accessory is a book.

Vivienne Westwood

Accessories are like vitamins to fashion.

Anna Dello Russo

Accessories! By shaping the silhouette, they make or break
one's style. As hallmarks of the designer, their personality is
always different from that of an outfit, either complementing
or clashing with it, and they can either affirm, emphasize
or destroy it.

Alber Elbaz

Cock your hat – angles are attitudes.

Frank Sinatra

Luxury bags make your life more pleasant, make you dream, give
you confidence, and show your neighbours you're doing well.

Karl Lagerfeld

If your pocket handkerchief is monogrammed, don't wear
it carefully folded to show the monogram peeking above
your breast-pocket. That's somehow ostentatious.

Cary Grant

Shoes and accessories are important to me because with these everyone is model size.

Karl Lagerfeld

My basics are black, white, or neutral, and I'll wear a ton of jewelry or carry a brightly coloured bag.

Rachel Zoe

At the risk of being accused of aristocratism, I continue to wonder why so very many people are proud to show off bags that display their maker's monogram. I can see one might think it important to have one's initials on things one is fond of (shirts, suitcases, napkin rings, etc.) but the initials of a vendor? Really, it's beyond me.

Georges Perec

I've always thought of accessories as the exclamation point of a woman's outfit.

Michael Kors

If I could be reincarnated as a fashion accessory, it would be a shopping bag or a white shirt.

Karl Lagerfeld

BAUBLES & BLING

I think jewelry can change an outfit more than anything else.

Iris Apfel

A many-stoned necklace of rhinestones for instance will look lovely with a décolleté frock for evening. It will go equally with a fine black knitted sweater for afternoons.

Christian Dior

Nothing is more deplorable than designers who indulge the imagination by aping reality. When a jewel is fake, it should be obvious from 20 metres.

Paco Rabanne

Big girls need big diamonds.

Elizabeth Taylor

The only word Elizabeth knows in Italian is Bulgari.

Richard Burton

These gems have life in them: their colours speak,
say what words fail of.

George Eliot

Dress suitably in short skirts and strong boots, leave your jewels in the bank, and buy a revolver.

Countess Constance Markievicz

I have always felt a gift diamond shines so much better
than one you buy for yourself.

Mae West

HATS

Wearing a hat is like having a baby or a puppy; everyone stops to coo and talk about it.

Louise Green

Life is like a new hat. You don't know if it suits you if you keep trying it on in front of your own mirror.

Shirley MacLaine

If a woman rebels against high-heeled shoes, she should take care to do it in a very smart hat.

George Bernard Shaw

So many hats and only one head!

Anonymous

SHOES

Whoever wears shoes knows nothing of how the barefoot suffer.

Chinese proverb

Unshined shoes are the end of civilization.

Diana Vreeland

High court shoes... they are sublime and yet also the most difficult shoes to make. Their line must be absolutely pure and must follow the curve of the foot... They elongate the leg, they're amazing.

Raymond Massaro

Men tell me that I've saved their marriages. It costs them a fortune in shoes, but it's cheaper than a divorce. So I'm still useful, you see.

Manolo Blahnik

You can never take too much care in selecting shoes. Too many women think that tbecause they are low down, shoes do not matter , but it is by her feet that you can judge whether a woman is elegant or not.

Christian Dior

Craziness in a shoe is great: you can have much more freedom, you can exaggerate and it doesn't feel stupid. But to have too much craziness near your face, that would just feel weird.

Miuccia Prada

Elegance is everything in a shoe.

Diana Vreeland

To wear dreams on one's feet is to begin to give a reality
to one's dreams.

Roger Vivier

The wealthiest woman in the world couldn't pay me to make
her an ugly pair of shoes.

André Perugia

Even more important, much more important than scent are
your feet. If your feet are correct, you have elegance. If you
haven't got the right foot – forget it. I mean you can have on
groundgrippers, if that's your line of country, or you can have
a foot problem, but there should be something absolutely
correct about the foot.

Diana Vreeland

If you wear shoes on your hands instead of your feet,
they don't wear out so quickly.

Pierre Dac

My shoes are gestures.

Manolo Blahnik

Women must be judged exclusively from shoes to hair,
rather as one measures a fish from tail to head.

Jean de La Bruyère

I can be
NAKED as
long as I'm
wearing the
right pair
of shoes.

Anna Dello Russo

DOGS

I don't care about the collection. My dogs are more important.

Valentino Garavani

Fashions in dogs change no less frequently that those for clothes
or hats. Greyhounds went out of style, with the exception of
Borzois ('as affectionate as a kitten, as brave as a lion'). They
were replaced by Sealyham terriers, Skye terriers and boxers;
nor should we forget the so-called 'aerodynamic' dogs –
Airedale crossbreeds, mostly – that were eagerly appropriated
by bourgeois young ladies, in the belief that their stylized
look was the perfect complement to their own personal style,
all discretion and falseness.

Irene Brin

Harry is a lot of work.

Dries Van Noten

This is my dog Moujik, painted by Andy Warhol.
Me, I'm Yves Saint Laurent.

Yves Saint Laurent, greetings card, 1991

I have two loves: one is fashion, second is Cucciolina.

Anna Dello Russo

If you are a dog and your owner suggests that you wear
a sweater, suggest that he wear a tail.

Fran Lebowitz

HAIR

Hairstyle is the final tip-off whether or not a woman really knows herself.

Hubert de Givenchy

Hair is magical, a musical adornment, and in the same way that musicians bring forth from silence melodies that remain fixed in the memory forever, hairdressers bring out of indifference faces that stay in the mind always.

Louise de Vilmorin

You're only as good as your last haircut.

Fran Lebowitz

Madame Schiaparelli, world famous couturier, claimed to despise hair: 'If women were intelligent, they would shave their head and paint some ornamental motif on top of their skull.'

Irene Brin

Never has hair been better dressed: waved, crimped, braided, pinned up in wings, swept back, twisted into ropes, with a truly wondrous skill. The Parisian comb is worth as much as a Greek chisel, and hair submits to it as meekly as Parian or Pentelic marble. Look at these beautiful black coils of hair, their pure lines set against a pale brow, and pressed like a diadem, by a torsade, which loops down and back from the chignon; this blonde crown, where a lovelorn breeze seems to flutter, making a halo of gold above a head of white and pink! See how tastefully gathered at the nape of the neck are these knots, curls, tresses wound like ammonites or the volutes of an Ionic capital. Could an Athenian sculptor or a Renaissance painter have arranged them more gracefully, with more ingenuity or style? We think not.

Théophile Gautier

If I want to knock a story off the front page, I just change my hairstyle.

Hillary Rodham Clinton

Having money is rather like being a blonde. It is more fun but not vital.

Mary Quant

If your hair is done properly and you're wearing good shoes, you can get away with anything.

Iris Apfel

I think that the **MOST** important thing a woman can have – next to **TALENT**, of course – is her hairdresser.

Joan Crawford

MAKEUP

The most beautiful makeup of a woman is passion.
But cosmetics are easier to buy.

Yves Saint Laurent

Well, she wore far too much rouge last night and not quite
enough clothes. That is always a sign of despair in a woman.

Oscar Wilde

With fine powder, women lend their skin a surface of
marble mica and take away from their skin the ruddy healthy
glow that makes our civilization appear coarse, since it
presupposes the predominance of physical appetites over
intellectual instincts.

Théophile Gautier

There is a shade of red for EVERY woman.

Audrey Hepburn

Treat your makeup like jewelry for the face.

François Nars

I think if women put some more of the time and money
they put on their heads in their heads, they'd be better off.

Iris Apfel

My top three beauty secrets are simple: always laugh;
always be yourself; always have confidence.

Donatella Versace

PERFUME

Thanks to the couture parfumier, perfume can be better than a note in the orchestration of elegance, it can – it should – represent the melodic theme, the light and direct expression of the trends and tastes of our time.

Colette

Fashions change and with rare exception are forgotten by the public. But the classic fragrances, like an invisible dress, endure. Fragrance must be introduced properly. A fragrance is like a signature, so that even after a woman leaves the room, her fragrance should reveal she's been there.

Oscar de la Renta

A perfume should be as imbued with meaning as it is light to wear.

Paco Rabanne

Perfume must not be linked just to fashion because that means that one day it will go out of style.

Thierry Mugler

Perfume is to be worn, like a second skin against your flesh, under a sweater. Perfume follows you, it chases you and lingers behind you. It's a reference mark. Perfume makes silence talk.

Sonia Rykiel

Perfume is a form of writing, an ink, a choice made in the first person, the dot on the i, a weapon, a courteous gesture, part of the instant, a consequence.

Serge Lutens

[Perfume is] that last and best reserve of the past, the one which, when all our tears have run dry, can make us cry again.

Marcel Proust

A perfume is an intimate object, it is the reflector of the heart.

Emanuel Ungaro

The man who pulls his perfumed handkerchief from his pocket gives a treat to all around whether they like it or not, and compels them, if they want to breathe at all, to be parties to the enjoyment.

Immanuel Kant

Fragrance is the first layer of dressing, a woman's invisible body suit.

Donna Karan

What do I wear in bed? Why, Chanel N°5, of course.

Marilyn Monroe

For a perfume to have staying power, it must first have spent a long time close to the hearts of those who created it.

Christian Dior

Just like men, perfume is never perfect right away; you have to let it seduce you.

Jean Patou

Perfumes are full of tricks and if you don't treat them with care, they will scatter your secrets to the four winds.

Louise de Vilmorin

A fragrance is like a cat burglar in your brain, it has the key with which to pick the lock and unleash your memories.

Roja Dove

Two things make women unforgettable, their tears and their perfume.

Sacha Guitry

What remains of a lover in the dark, if not the sound of her voice, the feel of her skin, and the impression of her scent?

Jean-Paul Guerlain

The beauty of fragrance is that it speaks to your heart... and hopefully someone else's.

Elizabeth Taylor

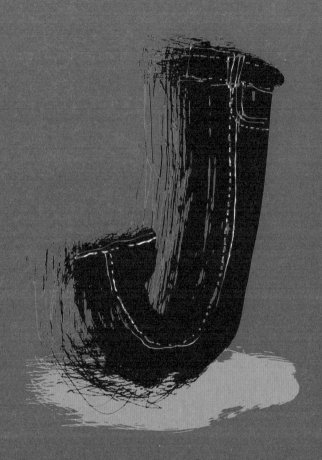

JEANS

Jeans! Jeans are the destroyer. They are a dictator!
They are destroying creativity! Jeans must be stopped!

Pierre Cardin

The only item of clothing that I would like to have invented
is blue jeans.

Yves Saint Laurent

Fashion is mysterious as a rule. Why are blue jeans classic?
You just hit on something that happens to be timeless and right.

Diane von Furstenberg

Blue has undoubtedly played a part in the global success of
jeans... Blue, this very particular colour, is ultimately the only
one that makes you dream. The colour of the sky, of eternity,
but light and easygoing.

Jean Baudrillard

We want to free jeans from the normcore hipster ghetto.
WASP jean styling is not the casual Friday cokehead banker
look. It is Tom Cruise exercising his virility.

Jean Touitou

The world changes, jeans don't.

Jean Baudrillard

Jeans represent democracy in fashion.

Giorgio Armani

Even though jeans suit me, I never wear jeans.

Carine Roitfeld

Three things: white cotton T-shirt, a pair of 501 Levi Strauss jeans, and a black cashmere turtleneck.

Ralph Rucci

I tend to splurge on fancy dresses because I always think I'll get a lot of wear out of them, but it's false logic. You should really spend more money on the things you wear every day, like jeans.

Alexa Chung

We made jeans to piss off the bourgeoisie. To break the rules. Now they've become a uniform. Our generation is completely screwed up. The proof is the fact that jeans are still around.

François Girbaud

Actually, blue jeans are the only thing that have kept fashion alive because they're made of a marvellous fabric and they have fit and dash and line... the only important ingredients of fashion. So I always say the same thing. I say: they're the most beautiful things since the gondola and leave it at that.

Diana Vreeland

You can be the chicest thing in the world in a T-shirt and jeans – it's up to you.

Karl Lagerfeld

I want to DIE with my blue jeans on.

Andy Warhol

HIGH HEELS

I'm not afraid of heights, have you seen my shoes?

Carrie Bradshaw, *Sex and the City*

Life is short, heels shouldn't be!

Brian Atwood

I would hate for someone to look at my shoes and say,
'Oh my God! They look so comfortable!'

Christian Louboutin

All I want are high heels, high heels. If I was a girl,
I'd wear a lot of high heels. High, stiletto heels.

Isaac Mizrahi

It is to the women of Paris that we owe the fashion for
slim high heels. The almost perpetual mud of the city made
them necessary: thin heels pick up less dirt and spread less
of it to the hem of the skirt.... Soon everyone noticed that
high heels gave sexuality to women's feet and made their
legs more elegant.

Restif de la Bretonne

I can see no reason why there should be danger from wearing
high heels. The great argument in their favour is that they are
prettier than low ones.

Sarah Bernhardt

If **HIGH HEELS** were so wonderful, **MEN** would be wearing them.

Sue Grafton

How can you live the high life if you do not wear high heels?

Sonia Rykiel

The higher the better. It's more about an attitude.
High heels empower women in a way.

Christian Louboutin

If I'm going dancing, then I wear the highest
heels with the shortest dress.

Kate Moss

Shoes must have very high heels and platforms
to put women's beauty on a pedestal.

Vivienne Westwood

High heels were invented by a woman who had
been kissed on the forehead.

Christopher Morley

Always wear high heels. Yes, they give you power. You move
differently, sit differently and even speak differently.

Carine Roitfeld

I've seen girls wearing high heels on the beach.
They were probably Russians.

Jean Touitou

The **ART** of
Seduction

Your dresses should be **TIGHT** enough to show you're a *woman* and **LOOSE** enough to show you're a *lady*.

Edith Head

THE FEMALE

New dress, new woman: good news.

Louise de Vilmorin

Feel like a woman, wear a dress.

Diane von Furstenberg

Fashion is killing women's body image of themselves.

Zac Posen

To be badly dressed is an impertinence for women.

Jules Barbey d'Aurevilly

I like being a woman, even in a man's world. After all, men can't wear dresses, but we can wear the pants.

Whitney Houston

Clothes are to women what herbs are to food: a small amount enhances the taste, too much disguises the true flavour.

Sacha Guitry

The woman is the most perfect doll that I have dressed with delight and admiration.

Karl Lagerfeld

There are thousands of reasons why women dress the way they do: and all those reasons are men.

Sacha Guitry

'In Paris, the war was scarcely over,' wrote Élisabeth de Clermont-Tonnerre, 'when there was a meeting at the Ritz where, for the first time, ladies of so-called good company rolled under the table, and this example was followed.'
Irene Brin

Remember, 20 percent of women have inferiority complexes, 70 percent have illusions.
Elsa Schiaparelli

The trouble with most Englishwomen is that they will dress as if they had been a mouse in a previous incarnation.
Edith Sitwell

I make clothes, women make fashion.
Azzedine Alaïa

Women dress alike all over the world: they dress to be annoying to other women.
Elsa Schiaparelli

Over the years I have learned that what is important in a dress is the woman who is wearing it.
Yves Saint Laurent

I *want* to see a collection for **WOMEN** who are going to the **MOON.**

Pierre Cardin

THE MALE

It is not possible for a man to be elegant without
a touch of femininity.
Vivienne Westwood

To be truly soigné, a man should never have fewer than
eighty suits.
Jean Patou

I think the way a man takes care of himself, of his external
appearance, his look, his clothes, is a mark of respect for
himself and of politeness towards others.
Jean Paul Gaultier

Any man may be in good spirits and good temper when
he's well dressed. There ain't much credit in that.
Charles Dickens, *Martin Chuzzlewit*

Besides, is our dress as ugly as it is claimed? Doesn't it have
its own significance, unfortunately little understood by artists,
imbued as they are with ancient ideas? With its simple cut
and neutral tone, it gives greater emphasis to the head, seat
of intelligence, and to the hands, tools of thought or signs of
breeding; it shows the true shape of the body and indicates
the sacrifices that are required for this purpose.
Théophile Gautier

A well-adjusted tie gives an aura like a delightful perfume to the entire outfit; it is to attire what a truffle is to dinner.
Honoré de Balzac

The well-dressed man is he whose clothes you never notice.
Somerset Maugham

Do you know why there are so many badly dressed people, Monsieur le Marquis? It's because they want to choose their own clothes instead of choosing their tailor.
Charles Ferdinand Humann, Parisian tailor of the 19th century

Dress up your sportswear and dress down your formal wear.
Luciano Barbera

Beauty and strength are no longer typical male traits in our era. Antinous would seem ridiculous today. The humblest jack can perform a Labour of Hercules. Therefore one should not adorn something that has no real importance; one should simply avoid clumsiness, vulgarity, inelegance, and hide one's body in an envelope that is neither too loose nor too tight, nor clinging too closely to the body's contours, the same for everyone, more or less, like a domino at a masked ball. No gold, no embroidery, no bright colours; nothing theatrical: one should be able to tell that a man is well dressed without being able to recall any details of his clothing later. The fineness of the fabric, the skill of the cut, the quality of the tailoring, and especially the way that all of this is worn – these add up to refinement.
Théophile Gautier

I believe men's clothes – like women's – should attract attention to the best lines of a man's figure and distract from the worst.

Cary Grant

At home, off-duty, I wear T-shirts from Fruit of the Loom – but I have them tailored.

Tom Ford

If a man tries too hard to be elegant, he veers towards the gigolo.

Giorgio Armani

Men are just as vain as women, and sometimes even more so.

Helena Rubinstein

MYSELF & OTHERS

Fashion must be the most intoxicating release from the banality of the world.

Diana Vreeland

When I first moved to New York and I was totally broke, sometimes I would buy *Vogue* instead of dinner. I just felt it fed me more.

Carrie Bradshaw, *Sex and the City*

It is said that a woman dresses for the people around her, for men, for her girlfriends. In fact, she dresses for herself.

Françoise Sagan

Girls do not dress for boys. They dress for themselves and, of course, each other. If girls dressed for boys they'd just walk around naked at all times.

Betsey Johnson

For both women and men, the clothes make the man. I mean that your mood changes according to what you're wearing, and you make a different impression on the people you're with. You express yourself through clothes.

Jean Paul Gaultier

On bad days, clothes don't matter. Days like that are for staying in a dressing gown. Putting on a dress has no healing effect on me. Same with makeup: if your skin is dead, so are your eyes. You don't fool anyone with the colour of your dress. When you have no sparkle, there's nothing you can do about it.

Catherine Deneuve

Fashion is the armour that lets you survive day-to-day reality.
Bill Cunningham

Fashion has to reflect who you are, what you feel at the
moment, and where you're going. It doesn't have to be bright,
doesn't have to be loud. Just has to be you.
Pharrell Williams

What you wear is how you present yourself to the world,
especially today, when human contacts are so quick.
Fashion is instant language.
Miuccia Prada

There are two main reasons why we wear clothes. First, to
hide figure flaws, of which the average person has at least
seventeen. And second, to look cute, which is at least cheering.
Fran Lebowitz

The most beautiful clothes that can dress a woman
are the arms of the man she loves.
Yves Saint Laurent

Clothes are a form of expression, of self-expression.
Catherine Deneuve

When you feel good wearing something, anything can happen.
Good clothes are a passport to happiness.
Yves Saint Laurent

If a woman smiles, her dress must also smile.

Madeleine Vionnet

Our minds want clothes as much as our bodies.

Samuel Butler

THE LITTLE BLACK DRESS

The zenith of elegance in any woman's wardrobe is the little black dress, the power of which suggests dash and refinement.

André Leon Talley

I love black dresses. I think everyone should own a lot, but black dresses don't sell online because on the computer they don't read like anything.

Tom Ford

The black dress is iconic because it emphasizes a woman's best qualities and smoothes out her faults. It is a magical piece of clothing that enhances a woman's femininity. It is the quintessence of chic!

Didier Ludot

Always have a good little black dress, pearls, and stay in the best hotel, even if you can have only the worst room.

Tilly Losch

A 'little black frock' is essential to a woman's wardrobe.

Christian Dior

The little black dress is the true friend. You remember when you met her... what happened the first time you wore her... she travels with you... is patient and constant... you go to her when you don't know where else to go and she is ALWAYS reliable and timeless.

Diane von Furstenberg

The little black dress must be luxurious, rich, sensual, diaphanous, exotic, severe, lush, demure, demanding, frivolous, amusing, and it must linger in memory, but above all, it must be simple and little and black.

Carolina Herrera

You have to wear black, aging or not, because when a little black dress is right, there is nothing else to wear in its place.

Duchess of Windsor

Scheherazade, that's easy; a little black dress, that's very hard.

Coco Chanel

I cannot forget Melina Mercouri in a black dress in *Never on Sunday*.

Jean Paul Gaultier

Here is a Ford signed 'Chanel'.

Vogue, 1926

The little black dress looks better in white.

Bill Blass

One is **NEVER** *over-dressed* or *underdressed* with a little black dress.

Karl Lagerfeld

CLEAVAGE

Having arrived at this temple of love, I chose the finest déshabillé. It is quite delicious, and of my own invention; it allows nothing to be seen, and everything to be guessed.

Choderlos de Laclos, *Les liaisons dangereuses*

I never wear a tie, because I believe when a woman gets dressed for the evening, she should leave at least one thing to the imagination.

Fran Lebowitz

It is from low-necked dresses that women's modesty, little by little, evaporates.

Alexandre Dumas, fils

The only place men want depth in a woman is in her décolletage.

Zsa Zsa Gabor

The greatest provocations of lust are from our apparel.

Robert Burton, *The Anatomy of Melancholy*

EROS & EROTICA

The fashion of sexiness and youth didn't come until the sixties
with the miniskirt and Brigitte Bardot before.

Karl Lagerfeld

I don't get the point of extreme sexiness. Except for prostitution.

Jean Touitou

I prefer spontaneous grace to premeditated seduction.
For me, sexy fashion always contains an element of calculation.

Kenzo Takada

Fashion cannot make you sexy. Experience makes you sexy.
Imagination makes people sexy. You have to train yourself,
you have to study, and you have to live your life.

Yohji Yamamoto

I've never understood sexy lingerie. I mean, what's the point?
The guy's only going to take it off.

Carrie Bradshaw, *Sex and the City*

I prefer to show the hidden body. I'm a man but I think that
what is on the inside is the sexiest. ...I don't like to show the
body ostentatiously. I prefer to dream.

Yohji Yamamoto

Fashion's
FOLLIES

Fashion is
a form of
UGLINESS
so intolerable
that we have to
ALTER it every
six months.

Oscar Wilde

FAST & FLEETING

One fashion has scarcely destroyed another before it is overturned by a newer one, which itself yields to the one that follows, which is never the last: such is our fickleness.

Jean de La Bruyère

Doubtless there is such a thing as pre-fashion, which comes first and makes a suggestion; fashion, which gains acceptance, and post-fashion, which with its excess condemns, and prepares for the advent of what comes next.

Marcel Rochas

Because fashions change, being themselves born of the need for change.

Marcel Proust

Deep down, fashion only has one adversary in this world: the metaphysician. In the name of fixed certainty, he objects to its movement and its restlessness. But in so condemning fashion, he also condemns life itself. Meanwhile, his colleague, the psychologist, who is not so fierce, ogles this fleeting goddess.

Francis de Miomandre

Fashion is like eating. You shouldn't stick with the same menu.

Kenzo Takada

Fashion is ridiculous before and after; it's only tolerable during.

Pierre Cardin

Why should man, however, who is forever seeking eternal and changeless values, be so concerned with surface and fleeting ones? Is there a changeling spirit behind the endless mutations of life itself? Perhaps the truth is that no form of expression by man can satisfy him. In art as in fashion, new styles or forms seem only a ceaseless and urgent search for some ultimate form of expression.

Cecil Beaton

Design should be a game for us, since fashion is not useful. But since the society we live in forces us to keep changing it, let's change it even more quickly, constantly inventing cool things, as crazy as possible! Basically I want to be an accelerator of decay.

Paco Rabanne

The changing of fashions is the tax that the industry of the poor places on the vanity of the rich.

Nicolas Chamfort

Today I don't like the dresses I liked yesterday, and I already adore the ones I am going to make tomorrow, but I avoid making anything just for the pleasure of making something new.

Marcel Rochas

Fashion is part of the daily air and it changes all the time, with all the events. You can even see the approaching of a revolution in clothes. You can see and feel everything in clothes.

Diana Vreeland

One consolation of fashion is that it gives you no time for regret. Your dress, Madame, is not yet faded before you put on a brand new one. And the old one, you don't even look at.

Francis de Miomandre

What goes out of fashion becomes custom. What falls out of custom is revived by fashion.

Jean Baudrillard

Every generation laughs at the old fashions, but follows religiously the new.

Henry David Thoreau

I **LOVE** the ephemeral: fashion is **MY** business.

Karl Lagerfeld

TRENDS & TYRANNY

Never be a slave to clothes, nor to body or soul.
Marcel Schwob

Like all tyrants, fashion only exercises its power entirely
over those too weak to resist it.
Honoré de Balzac

Fashion's authority is so absolute that it forces
us to be ridiculous at the risk of seeming it.
Joseph Sanial-Dubay

Those who make their dress a principal part of themselves,
will, in general, become of no more value than their dress.
William Hazlitt

Women who follow fashion too closely run a great risk:
losing their deeper nature, their style, their natural elegance.
Yves Saint Laurent

SHOPPING & SPENDING

I like my money right where I can see it… hanging in my closet.

Carrie Bradshaw, *Sex and the City*

Win or lose, we go shopping after the election.

Imelda Marcos

Women usually love what they buy, yet hate two-thirds of what is in their closets.

Mignon McLaughlin

Shopping is my cardio.

Carrie Bradshaw, *Sex and the City*

Buy less, choose well.

Vivienne Westwood

When I shop, the world gets better, and the world is better, but then it's not, and I need to do it again.

Sophie Kinsella

I do have a dominant shopping gene but, unlike a reasonable person, I never plan for what I need each season. I enjoy the thrill of the hunt, the discovery and the endless search. In another creation I was, perhaps, a hunter-gatherer.

Iris Apfel

Buying is not paying.

Louise de Vilmorin

REVIVALS & REVOLUTIONS

If one takes a slightly longer look at fashion, it is imitation that is its inspiration, its heart and its electricity. Without this imaginary carbon paper, which duplicates the slightest novelty like copies of a chain letter, there is no fashion.

Léon-Paul Fargue

Fashion is more usually a gentle progression of revisited ideas.

Bruce Oldfield

There's never a new fashion but it's old.

Geoffrey Chaucer

What is the true function of fashion, but to be a rehearsal for propagation?

Charles James

Fashion consists of imitating what at first seems to be inimitable.

Roland Barthes

POSTSCRIPT

There is much to support the view that it is clothes that wear us and not we them; we may make them take the mould of arm or breast, but they mould our hearts, our brains, our tongues to their liking.

Virginia Woolf

Sometimes I think I'm the last remaining person who goes to the shows for the pleasure of seeing the clothes, rather than desperately wanting to be there for the social side.

Grace Coddington

You cannot live your life in the elitist world of fashion and not step out or you're disconnected. You have to realize that fashion is not the endgame.

André Leon Talley

I loathe narcissism, but I approve of vanity.

Diana Vreeland

CREDITS